BEHIND THE
CIRCUS
scene

LIBRARY OF CONGRESS CATALOGING IN PUBLICATION DATA
Fenten, D X
  Behind the circus scene.
  (Behind the Scenes)
  Bibliography: p.
  SUMMARY: Describes the behind-the-scenes activities at a circus.
  1. Circus--Juvenile literature. (1. Circus) I. Fenten, Barbara, joint author.
II. Schroeder, Howard. III. Title.
GV1817.F46   791.3   80-14521

INTERNATIONAL STANDARD BOOK NUMBERS: LIBRARY OF CONGRESS
     0-89686-059-0 Library Bound   CATALOG NUMBER:
     0-89686-064-7 Paperback   80-14521

PHOTO CREDITS:

DX Fenten: Cover, title page, 4, 9, 10, 12, 13, 15, 18, 19, 20, 21, 23, 24, 26, 28, 29, 31, 33, 35, 36, 38, 39, 40, 41, 43, 45 top, 46.
Circus World Museum: 7, 8, 32
Ringling Bros., Barnum & Bailey: 16
Circus World, Ringling Bros., Barnum & Bailey: 45 bottom

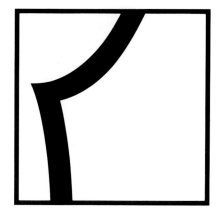

BeHIND THE
CIRCUS
scene

BY D.X. anD BaRBaRa FenTen

DesiGneD BY – marK e. aHLSTROM
eDITED BY – DR. HOWaRD SCHROeDeR
Prof. in Reading and Language Arts
Dept. of Elementary Education
Mankato State University

PRODUCeD BY – RanDaL m. HeIse

CRESTWOOD HOUSE
P.O. Box 3427
Hwy. 66 South
Mankato, MN 56001

Wild animals, no matter how well trained, can never be fully trusted.

The audience gasped, then became silent. Every eye in the arena was on the man in the center ring, every eye, including those of the tigers pacing back and forth close to the cage. This wasn't just another stunt. This was real. The animal trainer was in deep trouble. There were blood spots on his white uniform.

He was well into his act and up to this time all had been going well. The crowd loved the way he worked his animals. The lions went through their paces without a hitch. They growled, stood on their hind legs and pawed the air. They did everything the trainer had taught them.

Then it was the tiger's turn. After a few simple tricks, the trainer put a match to a large ring. It burst into flame as he held it high in the air. He spoke sharply to a large, fierce-looking tiger sitting on a perch. The tiger growled, sat back, then leaped through the ring of fire. The audience clapped and cheered. Slowly the trainer moved very close to the tiger. The tiger opened its mouth as the trainer moved his head closer and closer to the open jaws.

That's when it happened! Suddenly the tiger raised its paw and caught the trainer on the side of his face. The wound began to bleed.

The trainer's head was now between the tiger's jaws. The animal made a funny sound, like a sneeze. The audience held its breath, then started to yell for the trainer to get out of the cage. It seemed as if everyone had read the part in the circus program saying that to tigers, the smell of fresh blood is an invitation to death! Performers, musicians, stage hands and the manager were shouting to the trainer. However, he waved for them to be quiet. Again there was silence in the arena. Carefully the trainer removed his head from between the tiger's jaws. The tiger sneezed again. The audience cheered and clapped as the trainer bowed, holding a cloth to his face.

In just a few moments, the spotlight was off the trainer and he was helped to his dressing room. As the lights dimmed, the band struck up a different tune. They had been playing the famous march, "The Stars and Stripes Forever." Circus people know that when they hear this music there is serious trouble. As soon as this signal starts, circus people rush in to be of help. And, as soon as it stops, these same people fade into the background so the show can go on.

There is a great deal of teamwork in a circus. Though it may seem to the audience that all performers are only doing their own thing, they really aren't. Circus people have several things to do in each show, either in their own act, helping someone else, or as part of what circus people call the "Spec." This is the parade during each show in which almost all performers, helpers, and animals are specially dressed to make a truly "spectacular" sight.

The circus comes to town!

RIGHT OFF THE TRAIN

Long before any performance, the riggers and set up people must do their jobs. Soon after the elephants and other animals have been unloaded from the train cars, the set up crew starts its job. In the old days of real circus tents, elephants were used to pull and tug at ropes that lifted the tent and tent poles into place. Today there are only four of these tent circuses left in the United States. The other circuses do their setting up in arenas. Almost one hundred men, called riggers, take over the arena and put up trapeze riggings and high wires. Very few people who work for the arena help out. The circus people want to do it themselves.

Elephants and wagons battle through mud back in the "good old days."

"Riggers" put up, check and recheck every wire and and rope before the show goes on.

"We've been specially trained and have done it hundreds of times before," says the lead rigger. As he gives the rope a last tug and ties it to a stake, he shrugs his shoulders and adds, "It's our lives that are on the line, so we feel better if we do it ourselves." Though there are no longer problems of weather or elephants and wagons getting stuck in the mud, there are other problems for the riggers and their crews when setting up a circus in an arena. "For ex-

Special riggers must climb to the top of the arena to check trapeze and high wire riggings.

ample," said the director of operations for one large city's arena, "this place was a hockey rink on Saturday night. It became a concert stage on Sunday afternoon, and a basketball court a few hours later. After all this, the circus must open on Monday! Our people, together with the circus people, will have to lift the basketball court, melt the hockey ice, and set up an exciting three-ring circus."

Taking down, setting up, and rigging an arena can be dangerous work. However, injuries don't happen very often. "Planning is the key," said the lead rigger. "Long before the first act goes on there must be lots of planning. We must make sure that all the performers know where they are supposed to be, what they are to do, and when they are to do it. Our one aim is to make sure that the audience will really have a super time!"

PLAnnInG makes PeRFeCT

The large sign over the desk said, "The circus is the only fun you can buy that's good for you. Everything else is supposed to be bad for you." On the desk lay telegrams from all over the world, piles of handwritten notes and photos of circus acts. On a chair are costume sketches and a large calendar with airline tickets clipped to the edges. A young man is speaking on the telephone. "Yes, I know, the last few acts you told me about were great! I'd love to get to see the new ones you have now, but I just can't this trip. I'm booked solid to see some of the greatest acts in Europe. I'll get to you later in the year. Thanks for calling."

This young man is the producer of the circus and it's his job, among many others, to keep finding and signing up new acts. He says, "what I have to do is look for the best acts in the world. If I sign up a few new ones each year, the circus always stays fresh and exciting. We can't just sit back and wait for talent to come to us. We go out and find it!"

New acts, hoping for a chance with the circus, perform for the producer.

Covering about thirty countries and about 300,000 miles each year, the producer looks for acts in every corner of the globe. They come from small towns that don't appear on most maps, from countries that are rarely visited by people looking for circus acts, and from the famous circus capitals of the world. On any night at the circus, audiences see acts which have come from countries around the world.

Scouting for talent and finding it starts the wheels rolling for the circus producer. Now he must figure out how to best use each act. How might he show them off to best advantage? Where do they fit in with the other acts? What kinds of costumes should they wear? How many minutes can they

Acts come from all over the world to seek jobs with the circus.

keep the audience on the edge of its seat? What should their music be like? How should they enter and how should they exit?

Circus producers carefully plan each detail of every performance. They plan and work on all parts of the three-hour-long show until they hope it will please everyone in every audience. They know this goal cannot be reached, but keep planning, working, and arranging until they get as close as possible.

STAGERS AND CHOREOGRAPHERS HELP

Part of the job of being the producer of a circus is finding the right people for each job. Producers know they can't do everything themselves, so are always looking for people who can help.

Both the stager and choreographer work closely with the producer. They help create and put on the great shows and parades which have become an important part of many circuses. They must come up with ideas and themes for the giant spectacles, and turn out colorful, well-done acts. These must be planned to go along with special music and dances.

As the choreographer and stager appeared in the producer's doorway, he said, "OK, talk fast you

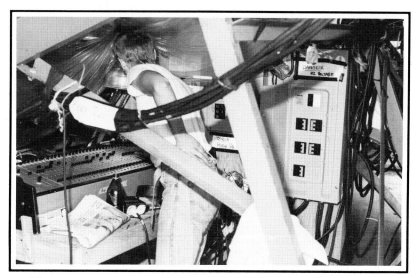

**Making sure the lights and sound are ready and working
properly is a big job.**

two. I have to be on a plane in about a half hour and
you know the traffic to the airport. What's the prob-
lem this time?''

The stager shrugged her shoulders and spoke
first. "Well," she said, "It's that new act. You know,
the one you liked and signed up right away in
Singapore. They just don't seem to fit in with the
rest of the show, we want them to parade in gold-
sequined costumes in the "spec," but they refuse.
They keep mumbling something about artists who
juggle people with their feet not having to march in
parades. Did you give them the idea they were so
special they didn't have to do what everyone else
has to do?''

Dancers line up for their entrance into the arena.

The choreographer nodded his head up and down. "That's only part of it," he said. "You know that as part of my job I'm supposed to teach dance routines to all the new performers. There's just no way I can teach these people anything. They keep acting as if they all had two left feet. They've made up their minds that they'll only do what they want to do and that's that."

The producer shook his head sadly. "I'll have a talk with them. If they don't shape up and fit in with the other people, they'll just have to leave. We can't afford to have temperamental artists with this circus. We all have to do everything and work together doing it. Maybe it was different in their last circus."

"Now, before I run and catch my plane, how's the new edition of the show coming?"

The stager and choreographer started talking at the same time. Both were excited with the plans for the new show. "It will," they shouted, "be the biggest and best circus ever."

JOYS OF BEING A VET

After talking for a few more moments, the two people left and the producer remained in his office. He started to straighten up his desk when another young woman came in and plopped down on the couch. "Hi boss," she said. "You know that trip you were about to take? I've got a feeling you're going to have to cancel. Half the animals around here are sick and the others look awful. We may need your help and your list of animal specialists."

Looking bothered and unhappy, the producer sat down again and mumbled something about the "joys of being a boss." Then he said, "You're the animal doctor. You fix them up. You're supposed to be the best in the business. I have to leave. If you've tried everything else, try some of those

Time for a big drink.

old-fashioned remedies. You know, like giving whiskey to an elephant with a cold. They sometimes work."

The doctor smiled and said, "You're some help. Along with all the other animals with prob-

Care of the animals is extremely important to the success of the circus.

lems, I've got two strange ones. The big chimp has a toothache and is biting everything in sight. He even bit my finger, and he likes me. And, get this, the giraffe seems to have a sore throat!" The doctor got up to leave and as she reached the office door turned and said, "Have a great trip, and don't worry. We'll probably get everything straightened out. See you later."

Costume designers make this performer and his horse come alive with color.

COSTUME AND SCENIC DESIGNERS

In another part of the office building, a different kind of meeting was going on. The people were kneeling on the floor surrounded by large sheets of drawing paper on which there were many large, colored sketches. The sketches showed circus people in beautiful costumes standing near, or riding on, all sorts of floats and platforms. These artists worked quickly and said little. Soon there was a sea of paper around the costume and scenic designers.

Beautiful floats carry the circus people in front of the audience.

This is the final stage of months of work. Hundreds of drawings have to be made before the first piece of cloth is cut and the first sequin sewed on. In a large circus there can be as many as five hundred costumes that must be designed and made. Each performer has several different costume changes and the animals, not to be outdone, have several blankets that must be changed during each show. Once these final sketches have been approved and work has started on the actual costumes, it can take as much as one hundred hours to complete some of the special costumes.

Costume designers have several matters to think about as they work and prepare for the tour. As an example, though the costumes must be pretty, colorful, and exciting, they must also be strong enough to stand the wear and tear of everyday use. Circus people are very superstitious and careful about the parts and colors of their costumes. You'll rarely see peacock feathers in a circus or the color green. Neither is considered good luck by circus people so costume designers don't use them.

Even completing a costume doesn't really mean it is ready for use in a show. When performers are going to wear a costume twice each day, and three times on Saturdays, it must fit well and be comfortable. If any part of the costume, from headdress right down to boots is in any way uncomfort-

The completed costumes must be tried on to make sure they fit and are comfortable.

able, it goes back to the drawing board to be fixed. Circus people are very careful about the way their costumes and their headdresses fit. If a headdress were to large it could throw a dancer or other performer off balance. This could be dangerous. In every case the costumes are worked on until the performer is satisfied.

It is not only the people who are considered when costumes are being designed and made. Animals also react to costumes. That's one reason why trainers wear new costumes in front of their animals many times before the real show. The animals must get used to any new look, new colors, or new fabrics. When they see these new costumes, they check them out by sniffing and sometimes feeling. If a trainer were to wear a new costume for the first time in a real show, it could startle the animals and there is no telling what they might do.

The same kind of care is shown by the scenic designer. It is very important that everything look well together and not clash. It would not be

This elephant seems to be enjoying it's new costume.

pleasant to see a large float that was mostly purple in color, carrying people wearing costumes of bright orange.

Another part of the scenic designer's job is to make the props, floats, and all the other gear sturdy enough so it lasts for an entire tour. The designer must also be sure that these things fit in, and out of, the entrances and exits in the many arenas the circus will visit. When the circus is ready to leave an arena, everything must fold down or come apart in small enough pieces to fit into its spot on the circus trains and trucks.

OTHER PLANNING SESSIONS

After much planning, the circus starts to take shape. It begins to look like a great show! Though the planners have been working hard all this while, it's time for the next group of behind the scenes people to take over.

The advertising and marketing people now prepare to tell everyone across the country that the circus is coming. They write newspaper, radio and television ads for each city the circus will visit. Then they try to get a few of the performers on TV talk shows to tell people about some of the exciting things in the show. Posters are printed for every city on the tour, and newspaper people are invited to see preview shows. The advertising, promotion, and public relations people work hard to fill every seat at the circus.

People in charge of arranging for routes and tours also play an important role. For months they have been working with all the arenas, or "houses," they will visit. They must agree on the amount of money they will pay each house, and those working as ticket takers, food sellers, and security people. The arenas must agree to the amounts of light, heat and air conditioning they will supply. They must also consider garbage and waste removal as well as the local laws. They check and double check all the arrangements to be sure the tour will run as smoothly as possible.

A circus is not a circus without lots of fun food.

The transportation directors do their job by seeing that everything can be packed on special trains, trucks, and vans. The general managers check out all details and plan the order in which the acts will go on. They also plan the length of an act, and what the people and animals should be doing when they are not performing.

STRIKE UP THE BAND

Until now, through all of this planning and preparation, there hasn't been a single note of music. Planners have been planning, performers have been practicing, and animals have been learning their acts. Not long after the circus starts to take form, the musical director starts to put it to music. Knowing that music is a very important part of any circus, and also knowing that music sets the mood for the whole circus and each act, the director tries to find the perfect music for every part of the show. High wire acts are more exciting, clowns are funnier, and acrobats seem more daring if the right music is being played.

Since most musical directors have been with the circus for a very long time, some as long as thirty to forty years, they know most of the music they can use. During the few months that the circus

Music directors and musicians work long and hard to find the right music for each act in the circus.

is in its winter quarters in Florida or other warm states, these musicians write music and words to fill the spots where new music is needed. Their heads are like giant computers holding long lists of all the circus music they've ever heard.

Now, with another season on its way, the director finds a seat in a rehearsal tent to watch both the new and the old acts. With the old acts he is trying to find the right music to keep the act bright and fresh. He must know if there are any new "bits of business" in the act and how to set them to music. For new acts, he must find the combination of tunes that will carry the audience through to the exciting ending.

He is busy jotting down notes all through this practice performance. "Start with a march to bring them on," his notes say, "then go into something softer as Janus climbs the twenty foot ladder sitting on Morro's shoulders. Quicken tempo a bit when Janus does handstand on top, and Maria and Dina lean off top rungs. Change to music with a fast beat as men balance tall poles on foreheads and women go to the top and move into their handstands. Swing into faster music as women, held to perches by only hand loops, whirl through the air. End of act. Music should leave everyone breathless."

After watching the acts and taking notes, the director moves along to another area where he must come up with music for some waltzing elephants, prancing horses, and a couple of cranky

Music makes the end of an exciting act even more exciting.

camels. He knows the importance of his music. The director also knows the truth about animals and music. People think the animals move in time to the music when it's really the music moving along in time to the animals. That's why music for elephants is slow, for horses, peppy, and for monkeys, very quick.

"DOORS, DOORS, DOORS"

When circus people hear the cry, "Doors," they know the audience is coming in to take its seats. It won't be long before the ringmaster steps into the spotlight and calls out to everyone in the arena, "Ladies and Gentlemen, and Children of all ages."

There's an excited hum as more and more people fill the arena. Vendors, called "candy butchers" by the circus people, are selling just about everything anyone could want. They're calling out their wares and their prices. Without moving from their seats the audience can get hot dogs, soda, ice cream, cotton candy, programs, popcorn, cracker-jacks, T-shirts, posters, flashlights on a string, and much more. Though most of the vendors work for the arenas, some circus people work as candy butchers to earn extra money. All vendors buy

Standing in line for the circus.

from the arena at a reduced price, sell to the audience at a higher price and keep the difference. If they have good items and really work hard, the vendors can earn a lot of money.

As the audience continues to pour in, the circus people go about their business. Many in the audience have gone through the "sideshow" before coming to their seats. Years ago, the sideshow was like a separate show and often required a separate ticket. It was sometimes called a "freak show" because it showed all sorts of people who were different from normal people. Very often there were midgets (as small as two feet tall), giants (up to about eight feet tall), and fat men and women (one of the most famous

The old time sideshows were often called "freak" shows.

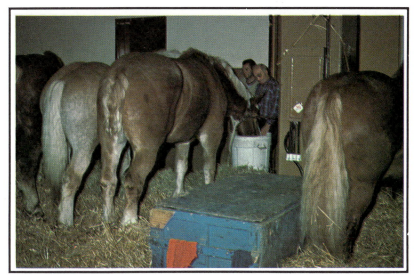

Performing horses don't get nervous. They keep on "eating like horses" right up to show time.

weighed over 650 lbs.). There were sword swallowers, fire eaters, and women with beards. Today all that has changed. Instead, it's more common for circus goers to see special performers breaking boards with their hands or bending bars of steel, as well as all the show animals being fed, watered and readied for their performances.

RIGHT BEFORE THE START

While people are filing by the sideshow, circus performers can be seen relaxing or getting ready to go on. A few at a time, the animals are also getting ready. Trainers and assistants are working with elephants, horses, llamas, lions, and tigers. At a quiet, spoken command, two huge elephants, after being unhooked from a heavy chain, turn and follow their trainer. Suddenly there's a lot of noise from the spot next to where the elephants had been. The trainer shouts a name, but the noise continues. A baby elephant is trumpeting, almost crying. She wants to go with the other two elephants. The trainer walks over to her. For awhile she is quiet. He turns to walk away and the baby elephant starts trumpeting again.

The trainer says, "wait," to the large elephants and walks back to the baby. The large elephants stand still and seem to sway back and forth. The trainer goes over to the baby, takes off the chain and says, "OK, OK. You're really getting to be spoiled. I was going to get you a littler later. C'mon now . . . now that you've made such a big fuss." The baby follows the trainer to the large elephants and they all walk down a ramp toward some large oil drums filled with water.

The elephants, including the baby, know what to do. They dip their trunks into the barrels and drink up the water. One elephant keeps throwing his head back until the trainer finally puts the watering hose into his mouth. When they're finished drinking, the elephants get a shower with the hose.

The trainer says to the largest elephant, "OK George, get those big feet in the air so I can wash your belly." When the large elephant lifts its front legs off the ground, the trainer hoses him down. Off on one side, the baby has tried to lift her front legs, but keeps toppling over on her side. In a few minutes, the elephants have been washed and scrubbed with a bristle broom. The trainer calls "tails-up" and the elephants follow him back to the stall, each one holding the other's tail.

During this time, all the other animals have been cared for, too. Some have been fed, others have been watered, and all have been cleaned. The animals sense that they'll soon be in the arena.

Workers prepare these lions for their performance.

Last
minute checks

Off to one side of the backstage area a family discussion is going on. Standing in front of some curtains used to make a dressing room, the show's star aerialists are speaking in both Spanish and English. It's something about schoolwork and, except for the two languages, it sounds like what goes on in many American homes. Called "The World's Youngest Daring Young Men and Woman on the Flying Trapeze," this family has been performing high in the air for a long time. The father serves as catcher for his three children who range in age from seven to thirteen. Under the watchful eyes of the father, the troupe performs all sorts of dangerous

"The World's Youngest Daring Young Men and Women on the Flying Trapeze."

flying feats. They do single and double somersaults and daring cross-overs from one trapeze to another. They do all the flying feats done by much older and more experienced flyers.

A little while ago they went out into the arena and checked every wire and rope they would use in their act. It looked like fun when the oldest boy jumped into the net from the trapeze and bounced up and down many times like he was on a trampoline. But it wasn't done just for fun. Checking the net is serious business. The net might save a family member's life if one fell during the act.

But now they had some extra time before they would go on. "Now you know the rule," the father said in Spanish, "no homework, no television. If you went to a regular school you would have to have your lessons in on time. Just because we travel so much and you learn through the mail is no excuse to be late."

The youngest boy, fixing the glittering silver belt on his white costume, looked up and said, "But Dad, there is a special on TV that we want to see. We'll catch up with our schoolwork tomorrow. Besides, why tell us about it now? We're almost ready to go on."

The father, in between slaps at his hands with a bag full of powder to keep them dry, shook his head. He understood the children's English, but always spoke to them in Spanish. It was his way of reminding them of their own culture. "Today," he said, "you do homework, tomorrow you watch television. Besides, tomorrow we must leave here. Did you remember that you asked to ride in the circus train instead of in our trailer? You won't do much homework on the train. Today you will do your homework. Tomorrow we'll worry about tomorrow."

mORe GeTTING ReaDY

All over the backstage area circus people were

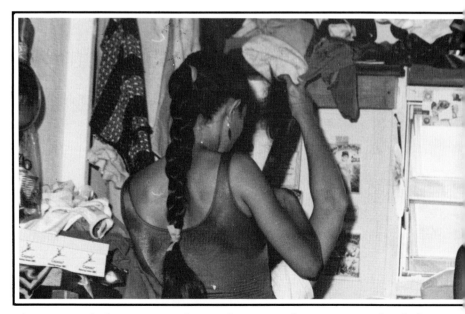

Circus people have to work together to make sure everybody is

getting ready or, if they were ready, were standing around chatting, having coffee or relaxing. One dancer, dressed in a short costume covered with shiny sequins, was leaning against a wall. A horse, led by a circus worker walked by, then suddenly stopped. When the dancer turned around, the horse pushed his nose against her and they stood together for a few minutes. She spoke to the horse and patted him as he nodded his head up and down. Then the horse was led away.

Lined up against the wall, in the order in which they would come out into the arena, were the floats and platforms. Circus repair people were tightening bolts, adding a bit of grease to wheels and getting

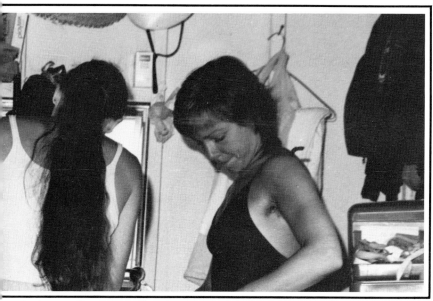

eady to perform on time.

Almost all circus animals become very friendly with the circus performers.

them ready to roll. A repairman was under one of the floats fixing the hitch. Only his feet stuck out and it looked like the float had feet.

In the far corner of this backstage area, men and women, who performed on huge horses, were limbering up. They jumped up and down, kicked the air, and ran in place. The horses stood in their stalls eating hay. In a very few minutes they would be on. They will be one of the first acts since they could get the audience in a happy mood. The crowd will cheer and clap as the troupe backflips from one horse to another while galloping around the center ring. At each turn around the ring, another person will be added to the human pyramid standing on top of two horses. A woman, the fourth member of the troupe, will reach the top and begin to juggle

Last minute checks and repairs are made on all of the circus equipment.

some flaming clubs. The audience will go wild! Just a few more minutes to wait!

There are only a few more minutes to wait for the other performers, too. The wild animal trainer talks to his cats as they lie in their cages. They seem sleepy, but get up when he comes close. The high wire walkers check their shoes and the bicycles that they'll ride across the wire. The acrobats lean against each other, pull against each other and jump up and down.

BRING ON THE CLOWNS

Close by, some other performers could be heard, but not seen. A section of the floor was enclosed by curtains to make a large dressing room. Near the slit in the curtain, which is used as a door, hangs a hand-painted sign which reads, "Clown Alley, Please Keep Out." Behind the curtains, the clowns are getting ready to go on. Several men are sitting at long tables which are covered with greasepaint, makeup, cold cream, funny fake noses, and wigs. They are staring into large mirrors and putting on their make-up. The dressing room is divided by a long piece of flowered cloth. On the other side of the cloth, a few women clowns made-up their faces.

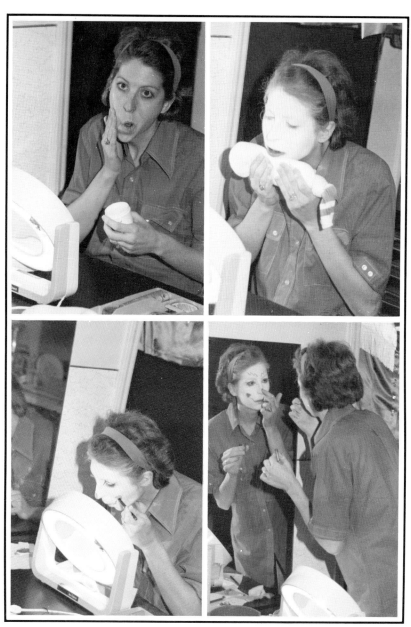

Make-up is serious business to a clown. It takes "Rainbow the Clown" over an hour to put on her clown's face makeup.

43

Costumes can be seen hanging everywhere in the room. There are also many props which will be used by the clowns in their different acts. Since they change costumes so often during the show and use more props than any other acts in the circus, it is easy to see why the clowns need their own private "world."

Each clown has his or her own special face make-up and costume which no other clown will ever copy. Like fingerprints, there are never two clowns that look alike. They take pride in their make-up, their "look," and try to make it better each time. Sometimes it takes a long time for a clown to put on make-up because there are so many things to do.

First, a clown makes sure his or her face is very clean. Next some cold cream is put on and then most of it is removed. Clown white, a sticky paste, goes on next, covering every part of the face and forehead. The hair is covered with a lady's stocking or a special tight cap. A few pats with a large powder puff covers the face with powder. Then red paint is used to make a funny nose and spots on the cheeks Many clowns make funny noses from liquid rubber or putty, or sometimes attach ready-made noses. Some of the noses even light up.

Mouth lines, eyes, eyebrows and eyelashes are painted on. Next it's time for a wig, a small hat, and the costume. The reason no one sees clowns

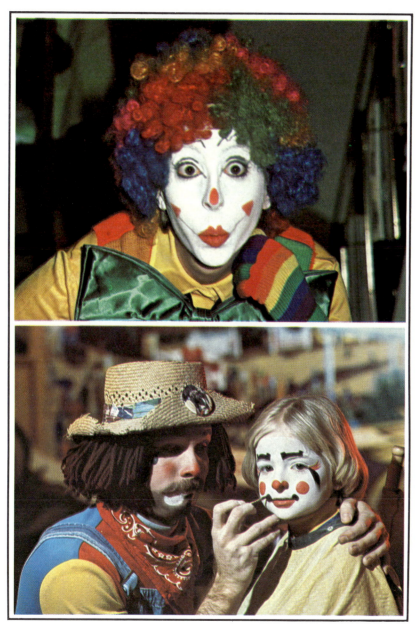

When your parents happen to be clowns, there's a good chance that you'll be a clown too.

before a show is clear. They're too busy putting on their make-up and costumes to spend time out of the "alley." It can take as long as one hour for a clown to get ready.

With only a few minutes to go before show time, several clowns come out. As they walk they are juggling some clubs back and forth. Soon they reach the spot where a vendor is selling circus posters. They keep juggling. One clown misses a club and it clatters to the floor. The vendor stops calling out about his posters and says, "Hey, could you two practice somewhere else? If I get hit with one of those clubs . . ." At that moment a club goes flying past the vendor's head. The vendor ducks as the club flies over. When it hits the

Just a little more practice before the show.

floor it doesn't clatter. It's not as hard or as heavy as the other clubs. It couldn't hurt anyone. The clowns laugh, grab their clubs and run back into the "alley." Once again they have played a practical joke on one of the circus people.

Clowns are always trying to have fun and make people laugh. One famous clown once said that to be a clown you had, "to be born with a funny bone." Whether that is true or not, people who want to be clowns today are usually trained at a clown college where the teachers are all clowns.

On WITH THE SHOW

The arena is now filled with people who are ready for a very good time. They know the circus is always different, exciting, and fun. The band begins to play. All the planning, practicing and worrying is about to pay off. The performers are ready and waiting. The riggers and other helpers are in their places on the floor of the arena. They'll do their jobs throughout the entire show. Without everybody helping one another there couldn't be a show.

The ringmaster steps to the center ring. The spotlight shines on him as he takes off his tall top hat and raises both his arms.

Ladies and Gentlemen and Children of all ages . . ."

FOR MORE
ADVENTURES
BEHIND THE SCENES
READ THE
COMPLETE SERIES:

BEHIND THE SPORTS SCENE
BEHIND THE NEWSPAPER SCENE
BEHIND THE TELEVISION SCENE
BEHIND THE RADIO SCENE
BEHIND THE CIRCUS SCENE

CRESTWOOD HOUSE
HWY. 66 SOUTH, P.O. BOX 3427,
MANKATO, MN 56001